For I praise young women twisting their wedding bands
        & old women with empty wombs & full
        shopping bags
For I praise crones with rouged wrinkles who shop in
        garbage
For I praise all women awaiting repairmen & all women
        who sleep with bottles
For I praise shopping carts & stirrups & ten-cent rest
        rooms
For I praise women who buy shoes which hurt & hats
        which are unreturnable
For I praise their outsides which become their insides
        & their insides which shall become their
        outsides

II

The Nose

The evidence mounts.
The bottles line up backward
in her mirror.
In each golden hollow floats
an embalmed homunculus.
Ambush.
Enormous dirigible roses
are blooming
in the corners of the room.
They float up
& explode against the ceiling.
Someone is planting orange trees in Versailles
& tending vats of perfume.
There's a tiger yawning in the four-poster
(reading 'The Story of O').
On the night table: Tabu, Russian Leather, Vol de Nuit.
'What makes a shy girl get Intimate?'

'There is only one Joy.'
& suddenly the gilded cupids
make obscene gestures.
She thinks,
'She looked deep into herself & found nothing.'
The mad-eyed violinist is about to seize
the lady pianist.
'Tigress,' he growls, 'Iced Tigress.'
'Toujours Moi,' she replies.
The country of the nose.

III

The Rings

After her husband died,
she had his wedding band
soldered to her own.
He was buried bare-handed,
slid into the earth.
Her hands move among the objects
which pretend to be my life.
She wears both rings on one finger.

Was it gold she sought to spare?
Or was she scared
of being married to a dead man?
How were their fingers linked?
Their mouths?
He was buried with his gold teeth on.
Darling, till death do us.

IV

The Dryer

Cleaned & peeled & sealed
down to her fingertips,
unable to touch
or smell herself,
her capsule stuffed
with thumbed copies
of 'Vogue' & 'Bazaar,'
her urine siphoned off
into the classified files
of the CIA,
her hair standing
weightlessly on end,
wind whipping
around her helmeted ears,
the first female American astronaut
is being launched!
She rises like Beatrice
into a sky
where all the stars
are Florentine gold.

No love is made
by touch in paradise.
Only the minds meeting
in concentric rings
of wind & bells,
only the legs of the compasses
meshing & turning.
Solitary mute,
always awaiting
the prince for whom
it will be worthwhile

to shake the meteors
out of her hair.
He comes.
He combs her out.
He's gay.

V

OB-GYN

Probing the long poem of her body
where she lies riding,
her knees framing his face,
her breasts & belly tented white,
he looks away
as if forgetting
that his hand
has disappeared.

It's dark.

He chatters about ski resorts.

Does she prefer Kitzbühel to Aspen?

He's touched some tiny town
high in the alps
where the sky sinks its blue teeth
into the mountains
& the sun slides down behind the peaks
like buttered rum.

A light goes on
in the uppermost chalet
above the tree line.
(Your ovaries are fine.)

Bring light!
A miner's hat or flashlight.
Is it like climbing Everest at night?
One false step empties you back into the sky?
What do the eyes of the fingertips hook on?
Skeletons from lost expeditions?
Babies with the faces of old men?
The womb blooming, a forest of peonies?

Not applicable.
Your poems are codes.
Pap. BI. CA.
Uptake. Follow-up.

You look away.

You tell me how expert you are.

I see that you stay upright
on the surface of the snow.

But I imagine how
the dark core of the mountain
sucks at your dreams
& I see you threading
a black forest
taking the curves gently
knowing it doesn't matter
if you ski through trees
easily looping left & right

Or falling
as if falling asleep
the shudder of your teeth
the spasm of your falling into her
moving through trees at night
moving through branches

Skiers above you
    charms on a long bracelet
        blue-faced angels
            angels in animal fur

            trusting the edge
        you leave
    no footprints

Living In
(my grandmother's house)

We entered you like a house,
blowing along
the white curtains.

In the kitchen
with its old aroma of pot roast,
in among the cannisters of tea,
the lavendered closets
with pillowed rows of pink soap,
boxes of cottonwool
& unfinished embroideries,

we said
how we'd like to be lived in
after our death.

Then we began to replace you,
seeping in like cave water,
changing your old order,
defending ourselves
with our own smells.

(I poured espresso
from your teapot,
hung black curtains
in your bathroom.)

Sometimes,
coming home suddenly,
I'd catch you,
your cheek as soft as willow tips,
shaking your head from side to side,
denying
the cancer that was eating you.

I knew
your ghost as my own wish
& wasn't frightened,
but you
refused to stay.

Now, armored by our walls of books,
paintings you wouldn't have approved
& foods you'd never taste,
we find ourselves
alone at last.

Yesterday
we visited your grave.

You were all there.

A Reading

The old poet
with his face full of lines,
with iambs jumping in his hair like fleas,
with all the revisions of his body
unsaying him,
walks to the podium.

He is about to tell us
how he came to this.

The Saturday Market

for Alexander Mitscherlich

Lumbering down
in the early morning clatter
from farms
where the earth was hard all winter,
the market women bear
grapes blue as the veins
of fair-skinned women,
cherries dark as blood,
roses strewn like carnage
on makeshift altars.
They come
in ancient rattling trucks
which sprout geraniums,
are stained
with strawberries.
Their fingers thick
& thorn-pricked,
their huge smock-pockets
jingling pennies,
they walk,
heavy goddesses,
while the market
blossoms into bleeding
all around them.
Currants which glitter
like Christmas ornaments
are staining

their wooden boxes.
Cherries, grapes –
everything
seems to be bleeding!
I think
how a sentimental
German poet
might have written
that the cut rose
mourns the garden
& the grapes
their Rhineland vineyard
(where the crooked vines
stretch out their arms
like dancers)
for this
is a sentimental country
& Germans
are passionate gardeners
who view with humanity
the blights of roses,
the adversities of vineyards.
But I am not fooled.
This bleeding is, no doubt,
in the beholder's eye,
& if
to tend a garden
is to be civilized,
surely this country
of fat cabbages
& love-lavished geraniums
would please
an eighteenth-century
philosopher.
Two centuries, however,
buzz above my head

like hornets over fruit.
I stuff my mouth with cherries
as I watch
the thorn-pricked fingers
of the market women
lifting & weighing,
weighing, weighing.

Student Revolution
(Heidelberg, 1969)

After the teach-in
we smeared the walls with
our solidarity,
looked left, & saw
Marx among the angels,
singing the blues.

The students march,
I (spectator)
follow.
Here (as everywhere)
the Polizei
are clean, are clean.

In Frankfurt,
the whores lean out
their windows, screaming:
'Get a job – you dirty
hippies!' Or words
(auf Deutsch) to that effect.

I'm also waiting
for the Revolution,
friends.
Surely, my poems
will get better.
Surely, I'll no longer

fear my dreams.
Surely I won't murder
my capitalist father
each night
just to inherit
his love.

Flying You Home

'*I only remember the onion, the egg and the boy.
O that was me, said the madman.*'

— NICHOLAS MOORE

1

'I bite into an apple & then get bored
before the second bite,' you said.
You were also Samson. I had cut
your hair & locked you up.
Besides, your room was bugged.
A former inmate left his muse
spread-eagled on the picture window.
In the glinting late-day sun
we saw her huge & cross-eyed breasts appear
diamond-etched
against the slums of Harlem.
You tongued your pills & cursed the residents.
You called me Judas.
You forgot I was a girl.

2

Your hands weren't birds. To call
them birds would be too easy
They drew circles around your ideas
& your ideas were sometimes parabolas.
That sudden Sunday you awoke
& found yourself behind the looking glass
your hands perched on the breakfast table
waiting for a sign.
I had nothing to tell them.
They conversed with the eggs.

3

We walked.
Your automatic umbrella snapped
into place above your head
like a black halo.
We thought of climbing down rain puddles
as if they were manholes.
You said the reflected buildings
led to hell.
Trees danced for us,
cut-out people turned sideways
& disappeared into their voices.
The cities in our glasses took us in.
You stood on a scale, heard the penny drop –
but the needle was standing still!
It proved that you were God.

4

The elevator opens & reveals me
holding African violets.
An hour later I vanish
into a chasm whose dimensions
are 23 hours.
Tranquilized, brittle
you strut the corridors
among the dapper young psychiatrists,
the girls who weave rugs all day,
unravel them all night,
the obesity cases lost in themselves.
You hum. You say you hate me.
I would like to shake you.
Remember how it happened?
You were standing at the window
speaking about flying.
Your hands flew to my throat.

When they came they found
our arms strewn around the floor
like broken toys.
We both were crying.

5

You stick. Somewhere in a cellar of my mind,
you stick. Fruit spoke to you
before it spoke to me. Apples cried
when you peeled them.
Tangerines jabbered in Japanese.
You stared into an oyster
& sucked out God.
You were the hollow man,
with Milton entering your left foot.

6

My first husband! – God –
you've become an abstraction,
a kind of Idea. I can't even hear
your voice any more. Only the black hair
curled on your belly makes you real –
I draw black curls on all the men I write.
I don't even look anymore.

7

I thought of you in Istanbul.
Your Byzantine face,
thin lips & hollow cheeks,
the fanatical melting brown eyes.
In Hagia Sophia they're stripping down
the moslem plaster
to find mosaics underneath.
The pieces fit in place.
You'd have been a Saint.

8

I'm good at interiors.
Gossip, sharpening edges, kitchen poems –
& have no luck at all with maps.
It's because of being a woman
& having everything inside.
I decorated the cave,
hung it with animal skins & woolens,
such soft floors,
that when you fell
you thought you fell on me.
You had a perfect sense of bearings
to the end,
were always pointing North.

9

Flying you home –
good Christ – flying you home,
you were terrified.
You held my hand, I held
my father's hand & he
filched pills from the psychiatrist
who'd come along for you.
The psychiatrist was 26 & scared.
He hoped I'd keep you calm.
& so we flew.
Hand in hand in hand in hand we flew.

The Book

I float down the spiral stairs
of the old apartment.
At the dining room table sit
my six ex-analysts, two brokers,
& five professors,
considering my book.
They dip the pages of the manuscript in water,
to see if it will last.

From where I watch, the sheets look blank.

They discuss my sexual hang-ups.
Why do I write about women
when, after all, they're men?
They enumerate my debts, losses,
& the lies I've told; the red lights
I have passed, the men I've kissed.

They examine a lock of my hair for bleach.

Finally, muttering, they rise & yawn in chorus.
They decide to repossess my typewriter, my legs,
my Phi Beta Kappa key, one breast,
any children I may have,
& my espresso machine.

My book, of course, is through.
Already the pages have dissolved like toilet paper.

I wake up with the bed
still on the wrong side of the dream.
My legs are scattered through the streets
like pick-up sticks.
Crawling on stumps, crawling
in the spittle & dog shit,
I bitterly accuse the City
& bitterly accuse myself.

How could I not have known
that the book was on the wrong side
of the dream?
How could I
have walked into it?

Where It Begins

The corruption begins with the eyes,
the page, the hunger.
It hangs on the first hook
of the first comma.

The mouth shuts & opens.
Newspapers are there & nursery rhymes.
Readers, lovers dangle
like Cassius, Brutus
from Satan's teeth.

The corruption begins with the mouth,
the tongue, the wanting.
The first poem in the world
is *I want to eat.*

The breast is the screen
of the dream;
no hungry poet
can ever be content
with two.

The corruption begins with the breasts,
the cunt, the navel.
It begins with wanting love
from strangers.

The breasts are two blind animals
with painted eyes.
The cunt is a furry deaf mute
speaking a red tongue.
The tongue is hunger.

The corruption begins with the curled snail
of the baby.
It begins with the white flood
of love on pages.

It begins with emptiness
where love begins.
It begins with love
where emptiness
begins.

Half-Lives

The notion of emptiness generates passion.
                    THEODORE ROETHKE

Seventeen Warnings in Search of a Feminist Poem

For Aaron Asher

1 Beware of the man who denounces ambition;
        his fingers itch under his gloves.

2 Beware of the man who denounces war
        through clenched teeth.

3 Beware of the man who denounces women writers;
        his penis is tiny & cannot spell.

4 Beware of the man who wants to protect you;
        he will protect you from everything but
            himself.

5 Beware of the man who loves to cook;
        he will fill your kitchen with greasy pots.

6 Beware of the man who loves your soul;
        he is a bullshitter.

7 Beware of the man who denounces his mother;
        he is a son of a bitch.

8 Beware of the man who spells son of a bitch as one
            word;
        he is a hack.

9 Beware of the man who loves death too well;
    he is taking out insurance.

10 Beware of the man who loves life too well;
    he is a fool.

11 Beware of the man who denounces psychiatrists;
    he is afraid.

12 Beware of the man who trusts psychiatrists;
    he is in hock.

13 Beware of the man who picks your dresses;
    he wants to wear them.

14 Beware of the man you think is harmless;
    he will surprise you.

15 Beware of the man who cares for nothing but books;
    he will run like a trickle of ink.

16 Beware of the man who writes flowery love letters;
    he is preparing for years of silence.

17 Beware of the man who praises liberated women;
    he is planning to quit his job.

The Wives of Mafiosi

Thinking to take on the power
> of a dark suit lined with lead
> of a man with a platinum mouth & knuckles of
>> brass
> of a bullet the color of a Ferrari

the wives of Mafiosi stay home
decanting the Chianti
like transparent blood.

They crochet spiders for the furniture.
They go to Confession.
They fill the ears of the priests
with mozzarella & nougat candy.

We too stay home
& dream of power.
> We sacrifice the steakblood to the dishwasher.
> We bring clear offerings of water to the plants.
> We pray before the baby pictures.

We dream of swallowing bullets
& coupling with money.
> We dream of transparent armor.
> We imagine we want peace.
> We imagine we are different
> from the wives of Mafiosi.

Anniversary

Every night for five years
he chewed on her
until her fingers were red & ragged
until blue veins hung out of her legs
until the children tumbled
like baby kangaroos
out of raw crimson pouches
in her stomach.

Now she was done.
She had once been a woman.
She had once sprinkled perfume
from the split ends of her hair.
She had once left a silver trail of sequins
in the moonlight
& slipped between the clouds.
She had once sucked
on inky fingers at school
& drawn a perfect india ink man.
She had once prayed to movie stars & poets.
She had once cried into the *Rubaiyat*.
She had once worshipped swizzle sticks from Birdland
& dreamed of a man with perfect teeth
& a wedding in a carved block of ice.

Divorce

Eggs boiling in a pot.
They click
like castanets.
I put one in a cup
& slice its head off.

Under the wobbly egg white
is my first husband.
Look how small he's grown
since last we met!

'Eat me,' he says agreeably.
I hesitate, then bite.

The thick yolk runs down
my thighs.

I take another egg
& slice its head.
Inside is my second husband.
This one's better done.

'You liked the white,' I say,
'I liked the yolk.'

He doesn't speak
but scowls as if to say:
'Everyone always eats me
in the end.'

I chew him up
but I spit out
his jet-black hair,
the porcelain jackets from his teeth,
his cufflinks, fillings,
eyeglass frames . . .

I drink my coffee
& I read the *Times*.

Another egg is boiling in the pot.

Paper Cuts

For Bob Phillips

Endless duplication of loves and objects . . .
THEODORE ROETHKE

I have known the imperial power of secretaries,
the awesome indifference of receptionists,
I have been intimidated by desk & typewriter,
by the silver jaws of the stapler
& the lecherous kiss of the mucilage,
& the unctuousness of rubber cement
before it dries.

I have been afraid of telephones,
have put my mouth to their stale tobacco breath,
have been jarred to terror
by their jangling midnight music,
& their sudden blackness
even when they are white.

I have been afraid in elevators
amid the satin hiss of cables
& the silky lisping of air conditioners
& the helicopter blades of fans.
I have seen time killed in the office jungles
of undeclared war.

My fear has crept into the paper guillotine
& voyaged to the Arctic Circle of the water cooler.
My fear has followed me into the locked Ladies Room,
& down the iron fire stairs
to the postage meter.

I have seen the mailroom women like lost letters
frayed around the edges.
I have seen the xerox room men
shuffling in & out among each other
like cards in identical decks.

I have come to tell you I have survived.
I bring you chains of paperclips instead of emeralds.
I bring you lottery tickets instead of poems.
I bring you mucilage instead of love.

I lay my body out before you on the desk.
I spread my hair amid a maze of rubber stamps.
RUSH. SPECIAL DELIVERY. DO NOT BEND.
I am open – will you lick me like an envelope?
I am bleeding – will you kiss my paper cuts?

Men

(after a poem called 'Women' by Nicanor Parra)

The impossible man
The man with the ebony penis ten feet tall
The man of pentelikon marble
The man with the veined bronze figleaf which comes
   unhinged
The man who's afraid to get pregnant
The man who screws in his socks
The man who screws in his glasses
The man who screws in his sunglasses
The man who gets married a virgin
The man who marries a virgin
The man who wilts out of guilt
The man who adores his mother
The man who makes it with fruit
The husband who never has time
The husband who'd rather have power
The poet who'd rather have boys
The conductor who loves his baton
The analyst who writes 'poems'
All these Adonises
All these respectable gents
Those descended
& those undescended
will drive me out of my skull sooner or later

Alcestis on the Poetry Circuit

(*In Memoriam* MARINA TSVETAYEVA,
ANNA WICKHAM, SYLVIA PLATH, SHAKESPEARE'S
SISTER, ETC., ETC.)

The best slave
does not need to be beaten.
She beats herself.

Not with a leather whip,
or with sticks or twigs,
not with a blackjack
or a billyclub,
but with the fine whip
of her own tongue
& the subtle beating
of her mind
against her mind.

For who can hate her half so well
as she hates herself?
& who can match the finesse
of her self-abuse?

Years of training
are required for this.
Twenty years
of subtle self-indulgence,
self-denial;

until the subject
thinks herself a queen
& yet a beggar –
both at the same time.
She must doubt herself
in everything but love.

She must choose passionately
& badly.
She must feel lost as a dog
without her master.
She must refer all moral questions
to her mirror.
She must fall in love with a cossack
or a poet.

She must never go out of the house
unless veiled in paint.
She must wear tight shoes
so she always remembers her bondage.
She must never forget
she is rooted in the ground.

Though she is quick to learn
& admittedly clever,
her natural doubt of herself
should make her so weak
that she dabbles brilliantly
in half a dozen talents
& thus embellishes
but does not change
our life.

If she's an artist
& comes close to genius,

the very fact of her gift
should cause her such pain
that she will take her own life
rather than best us.

& after she dies, we will cry
& make her a saint.

Back to Africa

*Among the Gallas, when a woman grows tired
of the cares of housekeeping, she begins to
talk incoherently and demean herself extravagantly.
This is a sign of the descent of the holy spirit
Callo upon her. Immediately, her husband prostrates
himself and adores her; she ceases to bear the humble
title of wife and is called 'Lord'; domestic duties
have no further claim on her, and her will is a divine law.*

SIR JAMES GEORGE FRAZER,
The Golden Bough

Seeing me weary
     of patching the thatch
     of pounding the bread
     of pacing the floor nightly
     with the baby in my arms,

my tall black husband
     (with eyes like coconuts)
     has fallen down on the floor to adore me!
     I curse myself for being born a woman.
     He thinks I'm God!

I mutter incoherently of Friedan, Millett, Freud . . .
     He thinks the spirit
     has descended.
     He calls me 'Lord.'

Lord, lord, he's weary in his castle now.
     It's no fun living with a God.
     He rocks the baby, patches thatch
     & pounds the bread.
     I stay out all night with the Spirit.

Towards morning when the Spirit brings me home,
    he's almost too pooped to adore me.
    I lecture him on the nature
    & duties of men.
    'Biology is destiny,' I say.

Already I hear stirrings of dissent.
    He says he could have been a movie star.
    He says he needs a full-time maid.
    He says he never *meant*
    to marry God.

Mother

Ash falls on the roof
of my house.

I have cursed you enough
in the lines of my poems
& between them,
in the silences which fall
like ash-flakes
on the watertank
from a smog-bound sky.

I have cursed you
because I remember
the smell of *Joy*
on a sealskin coat
& because I feel
more abandoned than a baby seal
on an ice floe red
with its mother's blood.

I have cursed you
as I walked & prayed
on a concrete terrace
high above the street
because whatever I pulled down
with my bruised hand
from the bruising sky,

whatever lovely plum
came to my mouth
you envied
& spat out.

Because you saw me in your image,
because you favored me,
you punished me.

It was only a form of you
my poems were seeking.
Neither of us knew.

For years
we lived together
in a single skin.

We shared fur coats.
We hated each other
as the soul hates the body
for being weak,
as the mind hates the stomach
for needing food,
as one lover hates the other.

I kicked
in the pouch of your theories
like a baby kangaroo.

I believed you
on Marx, on Darwin,
on Tolstoy & Shaw.
I said I loved Pushkin
(you loved him).
I vowed Monet
was better than Bosch.

Who cared?

I would have said nonsense
to please you
& frequently did.

This took the form,
of course,
of fighting you.

We fought so gorgeously!

We fought like one boxer
& his punching bag.
We fought like mismatched twins.
We fought like the secret sharer
& his shade.

Now we're apart.
Time doesn't heal
the baby to the womb.
Separateness is real
& keeps on growing.

One by one the mothers
drop away,
the lovers leave,
the babies outgrow clothes.

Some get insomnia –
the poet's disease –
& sit up nights
nursing
at the nipples
of their pens.

I have made hot milk
& kissed you where you are.
I have cursed my curses.
I have cleared the air.
& now I sit here writing,
breathing you.

The Girl in the Mirror

Throwing away my youth on duty
       on ink, on guilt,
       on applications . . .

I thought of you
       in your mirrored room,
       you with the huge open heart
       pulsing like a womb which has just given birth,
       pulsing like the beat in my head
       before a poem starts.

I thought of you
       & your charmed life,
       your hassocks, waterbeds & sliding mirrors,
       your closets full of beautiful faces,
       & your men, your men

the way you could open & close
       your legs without guilt,
       the way you said yes & yes & yes,
       the way you dealt death & regret
       as if they were cards,
       the way you asked nothing
       & everything came to you

Remember how we both loved
       that girl from the Kingdom of Oz?*

* Princess Langwidere in L. Frank Baum's *Ozma of Oz.*

She had thirty heads – all beautiful —
      but just one dress.

She kept her heads in a mirrored cupboard
      opened with a ruby key.
      It was chained to her wrist.

She had my heart chained to her wrist!
      I wanted to *be* her.

Though some of her heads were mad
      she could never remember which
      until she wore them,
      & one had a terrible temper,
      & one loved blood.

Can you imagine a girl
      who put on the wrong head one day
      & killed her body by mistake?

Can you imagine a girl
      who would not believe she was beautiful
      & kept opening her legs to the wrong men?

Can you imagine a girl
      who cut off her head
      to get rid of the guilt?

But no:
      you are lying in a room
      where everything is silver.
      The ceiling is mirrored,
      the floor is mirrored,
      & men come out of the walls.

One by one, they make love to you
     like princes climbing a glass mountain.
     They admire your faces
     & the several colors of your hair.
     They admire your smooth pink feet
     & your hands which have never known ink.
     They kiss your fingers.

You are everywhere.
     You can come all night
     & never tire.

Your voices mist the mirrors
     but you never write.

You have my children
     & they fugue the world.

Someday when my work is done
     I'll come to you.

No one will be the wiser.

The Woman Who Loved to Cook

Looking for love, she read cookbooks,
She read recipes for *tartlettes*,
terrines de boeuf, *timbales*,
& Ratatouille.
She read cheese fondue
& Croque Monsieur,
& Hash High Brownies
& Lo Mein.

If no man appeared who would love her
(her face moist with cooking,
her breasts full of apple juice
or wine),
she would whip one up;
of gingerbread,
with baking powder
to make him rise.

Even her poems
were recipes.
'Hunger,' she would write, 'hunger.'
The magic word to make it go away.
But nothing filled her up
or stopped that thump.
Her stomach thought it was a heart.

Then one day she met a man,
his cheeks brown as gingerbread,
his tongue a slashed pink ham
upon a platter.
She wanted to eat him whole
& save his eyes.
Her friends predicted he'd eat her.

How does the story end?
You know it well.

She's getting fatter
& she drinks too much.

Her shrink has read her book
& heard her tale.

'Oral,' he says,
& coughs
& puffs his pipe.

'Oral,'
he says,
& now
'time's up.'

Chinese Food

The mouth is an unlimited measure.
CHINESE PROVERB

WON TON SOUP

The soup contains something from each moment
of your life.
It is hot & sour.
There are islands of chives floating
like green ideas in the mind.
There is the won ton folded
like an embryo
skimming the water
waiting to be born.
There are the small unkosher bits of pork,
forbidden foods
which promise all the flavor.
There are the crystal noodles:
threads of silver light.

You eat your life
out of a skull-shaped bowl.
You eat it
with a porcelain spoon.
It is dense as water.
It is sour as death.
It is hot as an adulterous love.
& the pork – forbidden both by Moses & Mohammed–
is pink & sweet.

For the next course we chose
1 from Column A
2 from Column B
4 from Column C
& we passed the plates around
to share our lives.

We wanted to say: Look –
you taste my portion
I'll taste yours.

We wanted to say: Look –
I am dying of malnutrition.
Let's eat each other.

We wanted to say: Look –
I am tired of eating myself
every night
& every morning.
I am frightened
of my own mouth
which wants to devour me.
I am tired of the tapeworms
of my soul.

Belle ordered spareribs
sweet & sour.
'I have given my life to men,'
she said.
Like Eve in the garden
she chewed the rib
& regretted nothing.

Allan ate his beef with oyster sauce
& did not apologize
to Jews or Hindus.
'Sometimes food is only food,'
he said.

Roland ordered vegetables
& crunched
& spoke of meter.

Lucas ordered chicken
& denounced analysis.

Betty ordered dumplings
& defended it.

While Neal & Susan
dug deep
into their noodles.

I was left with sweet & sour pork,
haloed in batter,
glowing red with sauce,
slick as guilt
& sweet as smashed taboos.

Then we all poured tea.

FORTUNE COOKIES

The man who chews on his woman
will be poisoned by her gall.

The woman who chews on her man
will end her days as a toothless hag.

The poet who writes of food
will never go hungry.

The poet who describes her friends at table
will eat her words.

The poet who writes on rice paper
will nourish her critics.

A poem about food will not feed
the starving nations.

Your own mouth will eat you
if you don't watch out.

On the Air

[He] *went entirely mad and had the delusion his penis was a radio station . . .*

THEODORE ROETHKE IN CLASS, QUOTED
BY ALLAN SEAGER IN *The Glass House*

One toe
is the sensitive tip
of an iceberg,
& the moon sets
in my pinkie nail.
Every hair on my head
is transmitting signals.
My nipples give off
ultrasonic bleeps.

Only mad dogs
& lovers hear them.
Only distant poets
who are wired for sound.
He thinks his heart
is a receiving station.
His penis keeps on playing Rock & Roll.

I love a lunatic
whose feet are stereophonic.
His moustache tingles
like a tuning fork.
His fingers jangle
like a snail's antennae.
His navel rotates
like a radar screen.

Do you read me? Do you read me?
I keep asking.
When we're apart, when we're together
I keep asking.
& all the time he's spinning golden oldies.
His balls play Dixieland.
His foreskin honky tonk.

I play the engineer to his disk jockey.
I signal him to take a station break.
I ask him to identify the network.
I tell him to stop censoring the news.

It's Rock & Roll & Soul
& Body Counts.
It's pimple cream & soda pop
& jazz.
He thinks the FCC
has got his number.
He blames the President
when signals come in weak.
He thinks J. Edgar Hoover
sends him static.
& when he wilts,
he blames the FBI.

The Send-Off

For Patricia Goedicke & Leonard Robinson

(A letter to friends after sending the first book to the printer)

I

(Singing the Monthly Blues)

The book gone to the printer to die
& the flat-bellied author
disguised as me
is sick of the anger of being a woman
& sick of the hungers
& sick of the confessional poem of the padded bra
& the confessional poem of the tampax
& the bad-girl poets
who menstruate black ink.

I am one!
Born from my father's head
disguised as a daughter
angry at spoons & pots
with a half-life of men behind me
& a half-life of me ahead
with holes in my shoes
& holes in my husbands
& only the monthly flow of ink to keep me sane
& only sex to keep me pure.

I want to write about something other than women!
I want to write about something other than men!

I want stars in my open hand
& a house round as a pumpkin
& children's faces forming in the roots of trees.

2

Instead
I read my fortune in the bloodstains on the sheet.

3

What I wanted was something enormous,
a banyan tree
sinking its roots in the ground,
something green & complex as a trellis
eating the air
& the leaves uncurling their fingers
& the tendrils
reaching out for the wisps of my hair
& breathing the transformation.
To become a tree-girl!
with birds nesting in my navel
& poems sprouting from my fingertips –
but a tree with a voice.

4

I had imagined at least
an underground temple:
the Temple to Juno at Paestum,
the bone-jars & the honey-jars
& sacrifices sweetening the earth.

Instead: this emptiness.
The hollow of the book resounding
like an old well
in a ruined city.
No honey pot,
but another *Story of O*.

5

Sometimes the sentimentalist
says to hell with words
& longs to dig ditches.
She writes of this longing, of course,
& you,
because you are her friends,
write back.

6

She wants to write happiness books
with you –
big black happiness books –
because you tell her the moon's in your shoes
because you've taken off each other's socks
& counted each other's toes
& kissed
the spaces in between
because you fall (giggling)
into each other's books & find
the pages skin
because your laughter's the most serious sound
she's heard in years
because when she hears you making love
across the wall
you're singing
possible possible possible
while she sits here
in her big black book
beating her fists against the covers
loving the way she hates herself
much too much
to stop.

7

Here is the bottom of the pool
where the octopus
feeding on herself
vows to stop talking
about how
she wants to stop talking
about feeding on herself.

8

She is so bored with her notebook.
She has taken to writing in colored inks.
Green nouns. Shocking pink verbs.
Her notebook is a Mardi Gras.
The Rorschach on the sheet is brown.

9

She comes back again & again to this:
sex.
No matter how hard they mock her,
no matter what kind of cunt they call her,
no matter how shocked her father & mother,
caught in their cloud bed,
caught as in a primal scene
choreographed by Disney,
she comes back
to the dance
against death.

10

They are sitting in an office high
above Madison Avenue
speaking earnestly of commas.
He loves the way she uses them:

little hooks
to snare his shirt-tails.
But he proposes, tactfully, one semicolon.
Does he dare?
'I love your stuff,' he says.
Stiff blue pencil, he would fall on her,
revising everything.
Her paper dress tears off
& the layers of poems which are her skins
peel off.

She is a little font of tiny type.
She is ink.
She is that fine black trickle
running out the door.

The Age of Exploration

Sailing into your chest,
the white ship of my body
parts
the sun-struck water
of your skin
the silvery waves
of your hair –

a miracle!
the Red Sea parting for Moses –

& we ride
on a bed high
as the *Queen Mary*
& I straddle
your tall red smokestack
like the ocean wind
moaning
in mid-Atlantic.

All around us
people are waving good-bye.

Your wives bobbing in tiny lifeboats,
your children
riding on singing dolphins,
my mother

reaving the water
in an angry speedboat
& shouting warnings
through a megaphone,
my father
coolly shooting clay pigeons
from the burning deck,
my husband
about to harpoon
a great white whale . . .

Abandon ship!
Abandon ship!

We aren't listening.

Last lovers on the *Titanic*,
galley slaves transfixed
by the master's whip,
Jews in steerage,
Spaniards in search of gold . . .

You are the firehose
on my burning deck,
the radar
in my fog,
the compass
in my starless night . . .

You are the prow
of Columbus' ship
kissing the lip
of the new world.

The Tongue

I crouch under your tongue
like a lover afraid
of her own lie.
The tongue is the organ of love
& the organ of lying.
& the lie clings to the tongue;
the lie fills
the hungry mouth of the world.

I remember the sweet places
between your words
where my tongue probed.
I remember the brass clash
of cymbals
when your tongue
struck my nipple
I remember the purple sounds
of your tongue in my cunt.
Your tongue was the bell clapper
to my bell.

I remember your tongue
which rolled out
like a red carpet.
I remember your plushy royal purple
velvet tongue.
I remember your Nazi tongue

which hummed Wagner.
I remember your light & playful
Mozart tongue.

This poem is a gob of spittle,
a thin dribble.
It meant to speak all tongues,
it meant to sing.
But yours is in my mouth
& I am dumb.

Touch

The house of the body
is a stately manor
open for nothing
never to the public.

But
for the owner of the house,
the key-holder –
the body swings open
like Ali Baba's mountain
glistening with soft gold
& red jewels.

These cannot be stolen
or sold for money.
They only glisten
when the mountain opens
by magic
or its own accord.

The gold triangle of hair,
its gentle *ping*,
the pink quartz crystals
of the skin,
the ruby nipples,
the lapis
of the veins
that swim the breast . . .

The key-holder
is recognized
by the way he holds
the body.
He is recognized
by touch.

Touch is the first sense to awaken
after the body's little death
in sleep.
Touch is the first sense
to alert the raw red infant
to a world of pain.

The body glimmers
on its dark mountain
pretending ignorance of this.

The Cabala According to Thomas Alva Edison

All objects give off sparks

Your tongue, for example, enters my mouth
& sends electricity along my veins

When we embrace in your office, your secretary turns
    blue
As the base of a flame

Your fly zips up & down making the sound
of a struck match

Even a struck match gives off sparks

My nails on the back of your knees
give off sparks
your nails on my thighs

Thighs, in general, give off sparks
But even the fuzz on thighs
gives off sparks

Sparks, in general, make the world go round
(There are, for example, spark plugs)

Plugs, in general, give off sparks

In & Out: the current of the world

Paper Chains

The first snow of the year
& you lying between my breasts
in my husband's house
& the snow gently rising in my throat
like guilt,
& the windows frosting over
as if etched by acid.

You come from the desert
& have left a little sand
between my legs
where it rubs & rubs
& secretes a milky fluid,
finally a poem
or a pearl.

I am your oyster shell,
your mother of pearl
gleaming like oil on water
for two hours on a snowy day.

'Poets fall in love to write about it!'
I said in my brittle way,
& told you about other loves to tempt you
& heard your siren songs of old affairs.

I fall in love as a kind of research project.
You fall in love as some men go to war.

What tanks!
What bombs!
What storms of index cards!

I am binding up your legs with carbon ribbon.
I tie you to the bed with paper chains.

Gardener

I am in love with my womb
& jealous of it.

I cover it tenderly
with a little pink hat
(a sort of yarmulke)
to protect it from men.

Then I listen for the gentle *ping*
of the ovary:
a sort of cupid's bow
released.
I'm proud of that.
& the spot of blood
in the little hat
& the egg so small
I cannot see it
though I pray to it.

I imagine the inside
of my womb to be
the color of poppies
& bougainvillea
(though I've never seen it).

But I fear the barnacle
which might latch on

& not let go
& I fear the monster
who might grow
to bite the flowers
& make them swell & bleed.

So I keep my womb empty
& full of possibility.

Each month
the blood sheets down
like good red rain.

I am the gardener.
Nothing grows without me.

Going to School in Bed

If it is impossible to promise
absolute fidelity,
this is because
we learn so much geography
from the shifting of one body
on another.

If it is impossible to promise
absolute fidelity,
this is because
we learn so much history
from the lying of one body
on another.

If it is impossible to promise
absolute fidelity,
this is because
we learn so much psychology
from the dreaming of one body
of another.

Life writes so many letters
on the naked bodies of lovers.
What a tattoo artist!
What an ingenious teacher!

Is it any wonder we appear
like schoolchildren dreaming:
naked
& anxious to learn?

The Purification

Because she loved her husband
she found a lover.
Because she betrayed her husband with false fidelity
she went to bed with her lover.
Because she was no longer falsely faithful
she now felt honest.
Because she was honest
she told her lover she loved him.
Because she was honest
she told her lover she also loved her husband.
Because she was honest
her dishonest lover left her.
Because her lover left her
she felt betrayed.
Because she felt betrayed
she went back to her husband.
Now they had something in common.

Sleeptalk

Our dreams rise above our heads
& embrace

They ride together
in the ghostly trains of light
which streak across the ceiling

We sleep in their wake

A thin river of slime
joins our snail-mouths

Our eyelids twitch
the Morse codes
of our dreams

Our fingers clutch & unclutch
at the darkness

Palm upward to the stars
mouths shaping zeros
to the silence

Your penis rising
to conduct
your dreams

My moving tongue
still singing to itself

Three

The best lovers
think constantly of death.
It keeps them honest.
It causes them to make love all night,
avoiding sleep.

We made love all night –
we three.
You & me
& that death's head
which slept between us.
The third impression on our pillow
was death itself –
& I smoothed back your moustache
in the direction from which
it had grown.

All night you drank from me.
The light was bone white,
moon white, white as gravestones.
The sheets were limestone,
the blankets marble shrouds
& in the morning
we lay there quite as numb
as a sarcophagus king
& queen.

What a loving corpse you were!
I have known living men
to be much, much colder.

Being dead,
we needed so much heat –
that we rubbed each other's flints
& made blue sparks.

I think how valiantly we fought off sleep,
& of your skin
like worn-down marble.

I think especially of your gentleness.
Death also can be thanked
for that.

For a Marriage

(seven years old, just beginning)

After we had torn out
each other's ribs
& put them back –

after we had juggled thigh bones
& knee caps,
& tossed each other's skulls at friends,

after we had sucked
each other's blood
& spat it out,

after we had sucked
each other's blood
& swallowed it
licking our lips –

after the betrayals
& imagined betrayals –

after you left me in the snow
& I left you in the rain
& we both came back –

after staying together
out of lust
& out of fear
& out of laziness –

we find ourselves
entangled in each other's arms,
grown into each other
like Siamese twins,
embedded in each other
like ingrown toenails,

& for the first time
wanting each other
only.

The Prisoner

The cage of myself clamps shut.
My words turn the lock.

I am the jailor rattling the keys.
I am the torturer's assistant
who nods & smiles
& pretends not
to be responsible.

I am the clerk who stamps
the death note
affixing the seal, the seal, the seal.

I am the lackey who 'follows orders.'
I have not got the authority.

I am the visitor
who brings a cake, baked
with a file.

Pale snail,
I wave between the bars.
I speak of rope with the hangman.
I chatter of sparks & currents
with the electrician.

Direct or alternating,
he is beautiful.

I flatter him.
I say he turns me on.

I tell the cyanide capsules
they have talent
& may fulfill themselves someday.
I read the warden's awful novel
& recommend a publisher.
I sleep with the dietitian
who is hungry.
I sleep with the hangman
& reassure him
that he is a good lover.

I am the ideal prisoner.

I win prizes on my conduct.
They reduce my sentence.
Now it is only 99 years
with death like a dollop
of whipped cream at the end.
I am so grateful.

No one remembers
that I constructed this jail
& peopled its cells.
No one remembers my blueprints
& my plans,
my steady hammering,
my dreams of fantastic escapes.

& even I,
patiently writing away,
my skin yellowing
like the pages of old paperbacks,
my hair turning gray,
cannot remember the first crime,
the crime
I was born for.

Thirteen Lines for a Childless Couple

Because they thought always of the world ending
because he feared the whiplash of his father's sperm
because she feared the carriages & diapers
because she feared the splitting of her self
because she feared the world rushing in
because he studied little children

they never had children

Their child waited on skis at the top of a green hill
for the snowfall of his father's sperm

They huddled in the ski lodge drinking tea
& studying the cloud configurations

Eventually they died there

& the snow covered them

From the Country of Regrets

Those who live by the word will die listening.
DELMORE SCHWARTZ

It is a country where you can touch nothing: the food, the toilets, the people. The flies are everywhere. You come with your pockets stuffed with money, but there's nothing you can buy for fear of contamination, and nothing you can let touch you.

You enter a hotel with a central court. White plaster nymphs and cherubs in the fountain. Blue and yellow walls with white icing. Palms, ferns, growing out of white plaster planters. Servants sliding around noiselessly as if on invisible ball-bearings. Fans turning overhead. The constant continuo of the fountain in the central court. But the statues are sugar. Gradually, the water erodes them and they crumble and fall into the fountain. The fountain crumbles and falls into itself. The whole court dissolves. Next, it begins to dissolve the hotel and the guests, who are also made of sugar. The hawks circle and circle overhead, but they are not interested in melted sugar.

(Directions to the Ruins)

Where is the gate?
   It is a mouth with a tongue
   It is the curled tongue
   of the rain god

Where is the door?
>   Under the eyes
>   Behind the teeth
>   kissed with moss

Where is the roof?
>   Over the breasts
>   Under the sky
>   ruined

Where is the floor?
>   Fragments
>   A mosaic of a dolphin
>   The lost poems of the dolphin minstrels

Where are the birds?
>   Under the eaves
>   Under the stones
>   gone

Where is the altar?
>   Under the throat
>   Pitted with rain
>   slick with blood

Where is the tower?
>   Between your legs
>   Above the hill
>   falling

Where is the well?
>   Filled with the bones of girls
>   with gold   with blood
>   dry

Where is the tomb?

    Follow the signs
    Across the river
    above you

The taxis in this country are ancient American cars.
They start with a death rattle in the ignition. They puff
along producing a great deal of noise and very little
motion. Every thrust forward seems an immense effort.
On hills, the drivers and passengers have to get out and
push. These cabs are usually painted bright red or green.
The paint-jobs are amateurish and seem hastily done to
conceal the American paint underneath. Even the wind-
shields are painted red or green. Only little slits remain
for the drivers to look out. The interiors are covered
everywhere possible with transparent red plastic. It
hangs down in strips like old wallpaper. Glued to the
plastic are amulets of all kinds: blue beads against the
evil eye, Infants of Prague, fat-bellied Buddhas, Arabic
mottoes, St Christopher medals, homages to Quetzal-
coatl, tiny reproductions of copulating Hindu gods,
copies of the Lascaux animals, tiny plastic unicorns,
griffins, sea dragons.

It is difficult to communicate with the people because
every family speaks a different language, handed down
through the generations and kept within the family like
an heirloom. There are a few common words which the
whole populace shares: words for MOTHER, MOUTH, FOOD,
WAR; the verbs for MAKE, STEAL, BEAT, KILL . . . But even
these words have personal family equivalents which
people use in their own homes. A complete common
language is not necessary because incest is the rule in
this country, and children mate with their own parents
and never leave home. Their children, in turn, mate with
them, and sometimes even with the grandparents when

the grandparents are young enough. There are great numbers of deformed people and hemophiliacs as a result, and citizens with no birth defects are regarded with suspicion, as if they had some contagious disease.

(*Chant at the Body's Birth-gate or the Nunnery-door*)

Into the mouth

> lost lost forever
> & the teeth
> that prison

Into the eyes

> pull down the shades
> the brain still ticks

Into the nose

> hold it
> it stinks

Into the ears

> oh horny for music

Into the breasts

> dry as powdered bone

Into the navel

> flat
> no tunnel

Into the anus

> cities will die there

Into the cunt

> The cave of the mother
> let me lie down there
> rest
> let me rest

Tourists arrive in the country expecting a pleasant vacation, but within a few days, they are ready to leave. Generally, they fall prey to terrible diarrhea, or vomiting, or both. They try, despite their illness, to visit the great landmarks: The Temple of the Club-footed Virgin, The Cathedral of the Ebony Hermaphrodite, The Triumphal Arch built by King Akiliomoatli, who was born without arms or legs and invented a kind of primitive wheelchair called 'doabo' which many citizens still use. But sightseeing is soon made impossible by the constant bouts of diarrhea and the fact that public toilets are either very scarce or contaminated. A few enterprising citizens have made themselves rich by building toilet booths near the main public attractions and charging exorbitant rates to desperate victims. The people who have gotten rich this way are both admired for their shrewdness and looked upon with contempt by the rest of the populace – rather the way Jews are looked upon by gentiles in our culture. Often they become quite influential, but they are never allowed full equality in government and civic positions, and from time to time they are purged in pogroms (called, oddly enough, 'Regrets' – though it has no connection whatsoever with the English word, and has, in fact, a wholly different etymology). After these pogroms, the toilet booths are confiscated by the State and given to other citizens. These citizens then become part of the hated caste and in a few generations their descendants are purged, and so it goes. Tourists from our own country consider this horrifying and barbaric.

Invariably, tourists decide to leave after less than a week. They try to make plane reservations, but find the hotel staffs sullen and disinterested. The concierges shrug their shoulders and pretend not to understand when the tourists insist they want to leave. They go to the airline offices but find them always closed. They try to call, but none of the telephones work. Finally, in desperation, they pack and go to the airport.

The airport (which one scarcely noticed on arrival) proves to be one smallish room with peeling yellow walls, old American pop music (a woman singing 'Yes, We Have No Bananas' and a man singing 'Teenie Weenie Bikini' seem to be the only two records), fans turning overhead, and thousands upon thousands of mosquitoes. The wind riffles a five-year-old calendar with pictures of half-naked girls sitting on orange tractors.

A weathered sign labeled INFORMATION INFORMACION INFORMAZIONE hangs over what appears to be a counter. On closer inspection, one finds it is a bar, and those glittering objects which promised so much information are really liquor bottles.

An old woman walks by carrying a pillow in a soiled pillow-case. Except for her, everyone is in straw hats and sunglasses and leis and everyone is overburdened with piñatas, cameras, bottles of watered-down scotch, straw baskets, reproductions of ancient amphorae, straw flowers, skin-diving gear, guide-books, and pornographic postcards showing leathery-skinned peasant women fornicating with bored-looking donkeys before the ruins. Because of the mosquitoes, everyone is scratching ankles, knees, wrists. There is always a high whine in the air around one's ears.

(The Poem About Ruins)

It is your life which writes
the poem about ruins

     :

    It rises purple
    as a plumed serpent
    on a jungle coast

Its eyes are green

     :

    the veined wings
    of green insects

It worships sun

   :

    We are sitting our adolescence out
    here on the damp floor of a tomb

    We lie praying our hands like buried
     kings
    Moss kisses our genitals & lips

The poem about ruins
is inside us
trembling

   :

    It turns our cheeks
    slate blue

    No one,
    it tells us,
    can write it

Blank sun

I rest on the crumbled wall
of Caracalla's Baths

Something has dried the water up!

A butterfly lights on one shoulder wing

A Roman boy
would like to scrub my back

But my head is parched
                    :
                        The poem about ruins

We stumble through the labyrinth in Crete

Here Theseus fell
& Ariadne spread her legs
Here jars of honey stood
here jars of oil
a small way off
there stood the jars of bones

            Weeds sprouted from the furrows in my brow
            Rain pitted all the limestone of my cheeks
            The paint washed off as off the Parthenon
            My navel filled with earth

We are sifting through the stones
Ephesus, perhaps, or Ostia

Somewhere near some sea

There is a statue of my mother here
My father is the snake twined round her waist

                            Look down!

        We are climbing the Magician's Temple in Uxmal
        You cannot count steps up to the sun

We cling because we want to fall
& the poem about ruins
will be lost

Suddenly, everyone is herded into line for Customs and
interrogated severely. A number of people are made to
pay the last of their money as duty on articles they
brought with them. They argue with the officials, but
they cannot prove ownership and, in desperation, they
pay. When they return to their seats, some girls find that
their pornographic postcards have been stolen. They
want to complain to the authorities, but cannot remember any of the words for 'donkey.'

Finally, the plane is heard landing. The passengers all
run out to see it taxi up to the gate. It is a sorry specimen:
an old propeller plane with only three working engines
and no familiar markings. It bears a painted Dodo on its
flank and an Eohippus on its somewhat dented tail.
Several of the women become hysterical and refuse to
board. Children begin to cry. 'Teenie Weenie Bikini'
is still playing.

The crew walks out smartly. The captain appears to be
wearing a black cowboy suit from a 1940s Western, and
a black mask, silver spurs and six-shooters. The stewardesses are dressed like dance hall girls of the Old West.
They go over to the INFORMATION bar and order double
bourbons which they proceed to bolt down. All the
passengers watch them as they parade back across the
room and out to the plane.

There is much reluctance and shuffling around, but
everyone finally boards. The old woman with the pillow
is seen boarding last. The mechanics do a vaudeville
imitation of checking the engines, but the fact that they

are really not doing anything is clear. One propeller is still not working properly. It turns sluggishly. The takeoff is as slow as running in a dream. The plane seems to hover for a long time with its tail grazing the runway, and the tire treads screech at the moment of takeoff. Then, miraculously, the plane is aloft and hovering over the ocean. The seatbelt sign is still on. The pilot's voice is heard over the P.A. system: 'Due to mechanical failure, we will crash shortly.' The passengers sit riveted to their seats. Some laugh raucously. Others scream for the stewardesses. Others order drinks.

(*Invisible, with Stalled Engines*)

Perhaps we are not sinking
but God is going higher

He is finally invisible

Clouds pass above us
like milk in water

The sky is water

The plane we fly in
is a giant fish
which seems to stand still

But we believe in motion
we believe in the idea of motion

Forward, we say, is where
we are going

Perhaps God is going higher

We are not sinking
We do not believe we are sinking

Some young people are heard begging the stewardess for philosophical explanations. What have they done wrong? Why does evil have to exist? Why does death? Who willed it all? Doesn't the captain have any power over it?

The stewardesses bat their false eyelashes and smile their plastic smiles and ask: 'Milk or juice, sir?' Other passengers sit paralyzed, listening for messages in the sound of the engines. They believe their hearts and the engines correspond.

And there in the corner, writing about everyone, trying to separate herself out of the scene, or be above it, or control it, or pretend she dreamed it – am I. I am the one with the open notebook, the one who lost her pornographic postcards, the one with thousands of mosquito bites behind each knee. Nothing bad can happen to me. I am only collecting material. I am making notes: on hell, on heaven.

It seems as though we have been waiting hours for the crash, but this may be an illusion. The stewardesses have not served drinks yet. Perhaps they do not intend to because of the mechanical trouble. One cannot tell. Also, one cannot hear the engines for the singing. Strapped in our seats, suspended above the ill-fitting fragments of our lives, we are singing. There is no place to get to. The sun is setting below the horizons of our eyes, and all our windows seem to be on fire.

Loveroot

> *Run mad as often as you choose,*
> *but do not faint.*
>
> — JANE AUSTEN

> *Je cognois tout, fors que moy mesmes.*
> — FRANÇOIS VILLON

> *What I claim is to live to the*
> *full the contradiction of my*
> *time, which may well make sarcasm*
> *the condition of truth.*
>
> — ROLAND BARTHES

Dear Marys, Dear Mother, Dear Daughter

> *Mary Wollstonecraft Godwin*
> *Author of*
> *A Vindication*
> *Of the Rights of Woman:*
> *Born 27 April, 1759:*
> *Died 10 September, 1797*
> — MARY WOLLSTONECRAFT'S
> GRAVESTONE, PLACED BY
> WILLIAM GODWIN, 1798

I was lonesome as a Crusoe
— MARY SHELLEY

> *It is all over,*
> *little one, the flipping*
> *and overleaping, the watery*
> *somersaulting alone in the oneness*
> *under the hill, under*
> *the old, lonely bellybutton . . .*
> — GALWAY KINNELL

What terrified me will terrify others . . .
— MARY SHELLEY

I/NEEDLEPOINT

Mothers & daughters . . .
something sharp
catches in my throat
as I watch my mother
nervous before flight,

do needlepoint –
blue irises & yellow daffodils
against a stippled woolen sky.

She pushes the needle
in & out
as she once pushed me:
sharp needle to the canvas of her life –
embroidering her faults
in prose & poetry,
writing the fiction
of my bitterness,
the poems of my need.

'You hate me,' she accuses,
needle poised,
'why not admit it?'

I shake my head.
The air is thick
with love gone bad,
the odor of old blood.

If I were small enough
I would suck your breast . . .
but I say nothing,
big mouth,
filled with poems.

Whatever love is made of –
wool, blood, Sunday lamb,
books of verse
with violets crushed
between the pages,

tea with herbs,
lemon juice for hair,
portraits sketched of me asleep
at nine months old –
this twisted skein
of multicolored wool,
this dappled canvas
or this page of print
joins us
like the twisted purple cord
through which we first pulsed poems.

Mother, what I feel for you
is more
& less
than love.

2/MARY WOLLSTONECRAFT GODWIN & MARY
GODWIN SHELLEY

She was 'lonesome
as a Crusoe,'
orphaned by childbirth,
orphaned being born,
killing her mother
with a stubborn afterbirth –
the medium they'd shared . . .

Puppies were brought
to draw off Mary's milk,
& baby Mary screamed.

She grew up
to marry Shelley,
have four babes
(of whom three died) –
& one immortal monster

Byron & Shelley
strutted near the lake
& wrote their poems
on purest alpine air.
The women had their pregnancies
& fears.

They bore the babies,
copied manuscripts,
& listened to the talk
that love was 'free.'

The brotherhood of man
did not apply:
all they contributed
to life
was life.

& Doctor Frankenstein
was punished
for his pride:
the hubris of a man
creating life.
He reared a wretched
animated corpse –
& Shelley praised the book
but missed the point.

Who were these gothic monsters?
Merely men.
Self-exiled Byron
with his Mistress Fame,
& Percy Shelley
with his brains aboil,
the seaman
who had never learned to swim.

Dear Marys,
it was clear
that you were truer.
Daughters of daughters,
mothers of future mothers,
you sought to soar
beyond complaints
of woman's lot –
& died in childbirth
for the Rights of Man.

3/EXILES

This was the sharpness
of my mother's lesson.
Being a woman
meant eternal strife.
No colored wool could stitch
the trouble up;
no needlepoint
could cover it with flowers.

When Byron played
the exiled wanderer,
he left his ladies
pregnant or in ruin.
He left his children
fatherless for fame,
then wrote great letters
theorizing pain.

He scarcely knew
his daughters any more
than Mary knew the Mary
who expired
giving her birth.

All that remained in him:
a hollow loneliness
about the heart,
the milkless tug of memory,
the singleness of creatures
who breathe air.

Birth is the start
of loneliness
& loneliness the start
of poetry:
that seems a crude
reduction of it all,
but truth
is often crude.

& so I dream
of daughters
as a man might dream
of giving birth,
& as my mother dreamed
of daughters
& had three –
none of them her dream.

& I reach out for love
to other women
while my real mother
pines for me
& I pine for her,
knowing I would have to be
smaller than a needle
pierced with wool
to pierce the canvas of her life
again.

Will you change all this
by my having you,
& by your having everything –
Don Juan's exuberance,
Childe Harold's pilgrimage,
books & babies,
recipes & riots?

Probably not.

In making daughters
there is so much needlepoint,
so much doing & undoing,
so much yearning –
that the finished pattern cannot please.

My poems will have daughters
everywhere,
but my own daughter
will have to grow
into her energy.
I will not call her Mary
or Erica.
She will shape
a wholly separate name.

& if her finger falters
on the needle,
& if she ever needs to say
she hates me,
& if she loathes poetry
& loves to whistle,
& if she never

calls me Mother,
she will always be my daughter –
my filament of soul
that flew,
& caught.

She will come
in a radiance of new-made skin,
in a room of dying men
and dying flowers,
in the shadow of her large mother,
with her books propped up
& her ink-stained fingers,
lying back on pillows
white as blank pages,
laughing:
'I did it without
words!'

Elegy for Francis

Francis, the only pregnant white
whale in captivity, died last night
of internal poisoning in her tank
at the New York Aquarium at Coney
Island . . .
— The New York Times, May 26, 1974

Too big & too intelligent
to reproduce,
the ferns will outlast us,
not needing each other
with their dark spores,
& the cockroaches
with their millions of egg-cases,
& even the one-celled waltzers
dancing pseudopod to pseudopod,
but we are too big, too smart
to stick around.

Floating in Coney Island,
floating on her white belly –
while the fetus flips its flippers
in the womb
& she circles in the belly of the tank.

The last calf
beat her brains out
minutes after birth
& this one died unborn . . .

Fourteen months in the womb,
fourteen months to enter
the world of whaledom
through a tank in Coney Island.

Not worth it,
the calf decides,
& dies,
taking along its mother.

The whales are friendly, social animals
& produce big, brainy babies;
produce them one by one
in the deep arctic waters,
produce them painfully
through months of mating
& pregnancies that last
more than a year.

They croon to their unborn calves
in poetry – whale poetry
which only a few humans
have been privileged to hear.
Melville died for the privilege
& so will I
straining my ears
all the way to Coney Island.

Dear Francis, dead at ten
in your second pregnancy,
in the seventh year of captivity . . .
Was it weariness of the tank, the cage,
the zoo-prison of marriage?
Or was it loneliness –
the loneliness of pregnant whales?
Or was it nostalgia for the womb,
the arctic waste,
the belly of your own cold mother?

When a whale dies at sixteen hundred pounds
we must make big moans.
When a whale dies with an unborn baby
of one hundred and fifty pounds –
a small elegy is not enough;
we must weep loud enough
to be heard
all the way to Coney Island.

Why am I weeping
into *The New York Times*
for a big beluga whale
who could never have been
my sister?

Why am I weeping for a baby whale
who died happy
in the confines of the womb?

Because when the big-brained babies
die, we are all dying;
& the ferns live on
shivering
in the warm wind.

For Claudia, Against Narrowness

Narrowing life because of the fears,
narrowing it between the dust motes,
narrowing the pink baby
between the green-limbed monsters,
& the drooling idiots,
& the ghosts of Thalidomide infants,
narrowing hope,
always narrowing hope.

Mother sits on one shoulder hissing:
Life is dangerous.
Father sits on the other sighing:
Lucky you.
Grandmother, grandfather, big sister:
You'll die if you leave us,
you'll die if you ever leave us.

Sweetheart, baby sister,
you'll die anyway
& so will I.
Even if you walk the wide greensward,
even if you
& your beautiful big belly
embrace the world of men & trees,
even if you moan with pleasure,
& smoke the sweet grass
& feast on strawberries in bed,

you'll die anyway –
wide or narrow,
you're going to die.

As long as you're at it,
die wide.
Follow your belly to the green pasture.
Lie down in the sun's dapple.
Life is not as dangerous
as mother said.
It is more dangerous,
   ore wide.

For My Husband

You sleep in the darkness,
you with the back I love
& the gift of sleeping
through my noisy nights of poetry.

I have taken other men into my thoughts
since I met you.
I have loved parts of them.
But only you sleep on through the darkness
like a mountain where my house is planted,
like a rock on which my temple stands,
like a great dictionary holding every word –
even some
I have never spoken.

You breathe.
The pages of your dreams are riffled
by the winds of my writing.
The pillow creases your cheek
as I cover pages.

Element in which I swim
or fly,
silent muse, backbone, companion –

it is unfashionable
to confess to marriage –
yet I feel no bondage
in this air we share.

Becoming a Nun

For Jennifer Josephy

On cold days
it is easy to be reasonable,
to button the mouth against kisses,
dust the breasts
with talcum powder
& forget
the red pulp meat
of the heart.

On those days
it beats
like a digital clock –
not a beat at all
but a steady whirring
chilly as green neon,
luminous as numerals in the dark,
cool as electricity.

& I think:
I can live without it all –
love with its blood pump,
sex with its messy hungers,
men with their peacock strutting,
their silly sexual baggage,
their wet tongues in my ear
& their words like little sugar suckers
with sour centers.

On such days
I am zipped in my body suit,
I am wearing seven league red suede boots,
I am marching over the cobblestones
as if they were the heads of men,

& I am happy
as a seven-year-old virgin
holding Daddy's hand.

Don't touch.
Don't try to tempt me with your ripe persimmons.
Don't threaten me with your volcano.
The sky is clearer when I'm not in heat,
& the poems
are colder.

Statue

Cement up to the neck
& my head packed
with unsaid words.
A gullet full of pebbles,
a mouth
of cast concrete –
I am stuck
in a lovelessness so thick,
it seems my natural element.
My mouth closes
on stones.

Hand frozen to my chin,
my back a question mark,
my heart soldered
to its arteries,
my feet planted
in grass that cannot grow,
The Thinker ponders
ten more years of this:
a woman
living the life
of a statue.

Break free!
Melt the metal
in love's cauldron,

open doors, eyes, heart,
those frozen ventricles,
those stuck tongues,
those stuttering dependencies.
When the statue walks,
will the world dissolve?
When she shakes her shoulders,
will the sky shrug
& skitter off in space?

Or will the clouds cluster
to cover her,
& the blue wind gather
at her shoulders
& the men streak by
like jet trails in the air,
utterly ephemeral?

Playing with the Boys

All the boring tedious young men
with dead eyes & dirty hair . . .
all the mad young men who hate their mothers,
all the squalling baby boys . . .

have grown up
& now write book reviews
or novels about the life
of the knife-fighter,
or movies in which grown men
torture each other –

all the squalling boring baby boys!

I am not part of their game.
I have no penis.
I have a pen, two eyes
& I bleed monthly.

When the moon shines on the sea
I see the babies
riding on moonwaves
asking to be born.

Does everything else in nature hate
its mother?
Does the chick fling

bits of eggshell at the hen?
Does the pear spit
its seeds against the pear tree?

Who *made* all these squalling baby boys?

I am a reasonable, hardworking woman.
I sit at my desk & write
from eight to three.
When I emerge I do not ask your blessing.
What have I done but bleed
to get your curse?

Colder

Not that I cared about the other women.
Those perfumed breasts with hearts
of pure rock salt.
Lot's wives –
all of them.

I didn't care
if they fondled him at parties,
eased him in at home
between a husband & a child,
sucked him dry
with vacuum cleaner kisses.

It was the coldness that I minded,
though he'd warned me.
'I'm cold,' he said –
(as if that helped any).
But he was colder
than he thought he was.

Cold sex.
A woman has to die
& be exhumed
four times a week
to know the meaning of it.
His hips are razors,
his pelvic bones are knives,
even his elbows could cut butter.

Cold flows from his mouth
like a cloud of carbon dioxide.
His penis is pure dry ice
which turns to smoke.
His face hangs over my face –
an ice carving.

One of these days
he'll shatter
or
he'll melt.

Chastity

For Kristin Booth Glen

The sperm-smell of the mango
reminds me of how long it's been
since a man opened me up
& sucked my juice,
the sum of my parts
made hole.

I belong to a curious cult
of singing nuns.
We all have padlocked thighs
& knotted knees.
We work the beehive for ink
instead of honey.
& we hum like lovers coming
as we work.

Chastity!
Only the rankest sensualist
gives up sex.
The others never have to.
Men open me up too wide,
too desolate.
I've sworn off desolation.

The mango is a messy fruit to eat.
It covers the front of your dress
with yellow juice.
& strings of mango
hang between your teeth.
& all you're left with
is
a slimy pit.

Distrusting advice –
there is no one she wants to be
but herself –
although sometimes
she wishes
herself dead.

Who can tell her how to live?
Ms Lonelyhearts –
with her heap of red letters?
Doctor X –
with his couch shaped
like a coffin?
Mr Sex –
gimlet-eyed
cock-of-the-walk,
with his cakewalks & tangos,
his mangoes & bitter persimmons,
his helium balloons
bursting on branches
& his condoms
that glow in the dark?

No.
She turns her back.
Mistakes: she will make them
herself.

Love: she will choose,
like the rest of us,
badly.
Death: it will come
when it will come.

& Life: not reasoned or easy
but at least
her own.

The Woman of It

Your slit so like mine:
the woman of it,
the warm womanwide of thigh,
& the comfort of it –
knowing your nipples like mine,
& the likeness of it,
watching the mirror make love,
& the lovematch:
the mirror of you
in me.

I have creamed my hands
in the cave;
I have known my mother.
Years to get past
the barrier reefs of words.
We were natural together
as two little girls in the bath.
We hoped to be women someday,
we hoped to grow up.

Menstruation in May

Deaths & betrayals,
a friend having her breasts cut off,
a friend having his heart re-wired,
a husband lying,
a lover never writing,
& all this in the middle of May.

I walk out into the green wind of Spring.
The air whistles at my calves
like silk stockings –
my grandmother's silk stockings
kept in a drawer –
& whispering songs of the twenties.

My breasts ache,
my heart skips over cracks,
my womb pulls earthward
with its heavy blood.
I seem to be attached to those I love
by chains of flesh.
Perhaps the mind lacks empathy enough;
the body has to bleed as well.

I can't imagine them cutting you apart –
I with my endless dreams of torture,
who lay awake nights with my eyelids screaming
all childhood long.

I never saw your breasts
yet can't imagine you without them.
All week I have been fondling my nipples,
half in terror, half in pleasure.
Stay, flesh, stay.
If it is all we have,
especially,
stay.

Is there a poetry of blood
where lines are arms lopped off
& stanzas are whole bodies opened wide?
Is there an art which pains us
just like life?

I squeeze my breast
for the invisible ink of milk.
I bear down hard –
no baby's head appears.

The poems keep flowing monthly
like my blood.

The word is flesh, I say,
still unconvinced.

The flesh is flesh.
The word is on its own.

Fugue for Three Hands & Ornate Bedstead

For Jill Robinson

> *The only way for a relationship to survive,*
> *I think, is to have no sex at all. After all,*
> *you marry for friendship, for companion-*
> *ship – and passion after a while . . .*
> *pfffft. I mean, does it excite you when your*
> *left hand touches your right?*
> — DIANE VON UND ZU FÜRSTENBERG,
> *New York* Magazine, February 5, 1973

Pfffft.
My left hand is touching my right
after seven years
of marriage.

Donne's lovers' hands
cemented by their sweat
the stars of star-crossed lovers
whose life-lines
cross each other out –
could not be more electric
than these hands
making love from left to right

I hate to come right out & say this
& seem dull,
but I get excited
when my left hand strokes my right.

The right hand holds the pen
& feels the cramp,
while the cool & lucid
sinister left hand
makes love with silent finger-pads & palm
& helps the other write.

What friendship
after years of breaking bread!
These hands have gone to table
& to bed
for seven years
& they are still not severed.

They sweat, they freeze, they chap,
they crack their knuckles.
They tie each other's ties.
& buckle buckles.
& yet these hands are friends
when all is done
& when it comes to passion
they aren't numb.

Occasionally, it's true,
one needs a friend –
a hairy, unfamiliar
helping hand.

If two is company
can three be ecstasy?

But what is the sound
of three hands clapping?

Penis Envy

I envy men who can yearn
with infinite emptiness
toward the body of a woman,

hoping that the yearning
will make a child,
that the emptiness itself
will fertilize the darkness.

Women have no illusions about this,
being at once
houses, tunnels,
cups & cupbearers,
knowing emptiness as a temporary state
between two fullnesses,
& seeing no romance in it.

If I were a man
doomed to that infinite emptiness,
& having no choice in the matter,
I would, like the rest, no doubt,
find a woman
& christen her moonbelly,
madonna, gold-haired goddess
& make her the tent of my longing,
the silk parachute of my lust,
the blue-eyed icon of my sacred sexual itch,
the mother of my hunger.

But since I am a woman,
I must not only inspire the poem
but also type it,
not only conceive the child
but also bear it,
not only bear the child
but also bathe it,
not only bathe the child
but also feed it,
not only feed the child
but also carry it
everywhere, everywhere . . .

while men write poems
on the mysteries of motherhood.

I envy men who can yearn
with infinite emptiness.

In the Penile Colony

For Bob Phillips

Wearing my familiar worry wrapped
around me like a fur coat,
I walk out into the transatlantic air,
endangered species,
womankind in a world
of shivering men.

Kindness, worry, anxiousness-to-please
have been my nursemaids;
fear has suckled me
since I first learned to breathe.

But now the streets are strewn with beggarmen
who kneel
clutching tin cups & pencils,
strutting on their stumps
where legs once grew.

This is a curious world
changing so fast
that we are all babies
born in taxicabs.

That first great gust of air
which fills our lungs
turns blood from iron red
to inky black –
& never back.

A street of stumps?
A forest thick with cocks?
'Alice lost in the pénile colony' –
you said.
But the forest is dying
(Uncle Vanya knew)
& see how those trees
bend & whimper
under their own dry rot.

Dying,
they want to kill us.
('Don't take it personally,'
the murderer said.)

We women will have to shed
our wraps of fear.
Kindness, worry, anxiousness-to-please
are luxuries our kind can no more wear
than fur coats.

In a rotting forest,
we are lumberjacks
raising our double axes . . .

Tapestry, with Unicorn

What we were searching for
did not, of course, exist –
that tapestried morning,
under those woven clouds
where impossible birds
sang quite incredibly
of unattainable things.

A moth among the dandelions
warbled like the nightingale of Keats,
& trochees sang among the iambs,
while you in your curled collar & brocaded vest,
were beaming down the sun-strewn silken grass
where I lay in a frenzy of ruffles,
ear pressed to the earth
so I might hear –
the echoing hoofbeats of the unicorn.

He came in a blaze
of embroidered glory, with agate eyes
and his infamous ivory horn
blaring baroque concerti –
& thinking to have captured him for good,
we toasted in white wine and wafers,
and took, before witnesses,
impossible vows.

The rest you know:
how in the toadstool damp of evening
where lovers toss and cough,
speaking to each other
in the thick syllables of sleep,
through the long winter's night of marriage,
the unicorn slips away,
& love, like an insomniac's nightmare,
becomes only
the lesser of two evils.

Sometimes he comes again,
thrashing through the tapestried dark,
uprooting limbs & sheets
& finespun wisps of hair.
But the quest having been forgotten,
we do not know him,
or else we call him
by a different name.

You Whom I Hoped to Reach by Writing

You whom I hoped to reach by writing,
you beyond the multicolored tangle
of telephone wires,
you with your white paper soul
trampled in transit,
you with kaleidoscope stamps
& black cancellations,
you who put your finger on my heart as I slept,
you whom I jostle in elevators,
you whom I stare at in subways,
you shopping for love in department stores . . .

I write to you
& someone else answers:
the man who hates his wife
& wants to meet me,
the girl who mistakes me for mother . . .
My strange vocation
is to be paid for my nightmares.

I write to you, my love,
& someone else
always answers.

Sunjuice

What happens when the juice of the sun
drenches you
with its lemony tang, its tart sweetness
& your whole body stings with singing
so that your toes sing to your mouth
& your navel whistles to your breasts
& your breasts wave to everyone
as you walk down the summer street?

What will you do
when nothing will do
but to throw your arms around trees
& men
& to greet every woman as sister
& to run naked in the spray of the fire hydrants
with children of assorted colors?

Will you cover your drenched skin
with woolen clothes?
Will you wear a diaper of herringbone tweed?
Will you piece together a shroud of figleaves
& lecture at the University
on the Lives of the Major Poets,
the History of Despair in Art?

Catching Up

We sit on a rock
to allow our souls
to catch up with us.

We have been traveling
a long time.

Behind us are forests of books
with pages green as leaves.
A blood sun stares
over the horizon.

Our souls are slow.
They walk miles behind
our long shadows.

They do not dance.
They need all their strength
merely to follow us.

Sometimes we run too fast
or trip climbing
the rotten rungs
in fame's ladder.

Our souls know
it leads nowhere.

They are not afraid
of losing us.

Unblocked

I had not written a poem in months,
my mouth was dry,
full of old newspaper clippings
& book reviews
& articles on the Sum Total
of Art.

Dead,
unable to write,
I had become my critics.
My passion was punished
with staleness,
my lust had turned
to printer's ink
on dust.

Then you appeared,
seized me quite suddenly
one night in the midst of a lecture,
bound my hands with rubber bands,
paper-clipped my nipples,
wrote your terrible lust on my belly,
your tenderness on my cheeks.

I felt that fatal spasm of love
& lost my dinner.
I felt that hunger for you
& I had diarrhea.

Oh, I know my cynical readers,
my cynical selves . . .
but the Muse winged over the toilet
& smelled the shit.
& the Muse flew up my ass
that fateful night
& now I am sick again
& now can write.

The Hole

She is frightened when the book is done.
The novel whose scrawled yellow pages
have filled her heart for seven years
is snatched away.
& the hole in her heart echoes
like a garbage can
thrown against a courtyard
in New York.

She writes to fill that hole
whose quicksand edges
eat her heart out from the muddy center,
& when they take away her pages,
her stuffing, her asbestos insulation,
she rattles
like a palsied hand
sticking out a silver spoon
for sugar.

The book-in-progress
was the mattress of a bed
where her past made love
to her future,
where her mother hugged her father,

where all the apparitions of the dead
slept like babies
after nighttime bottles.

She has no choice – she will begin again.
Her loneliness: the motor of her pen.

Eating Death, For Anne Sexton

My dearest Anne,
I am living by a lake
with a young man
I met one week after you died.

His beard is red,
his eyes flicker like cat's eyes,
& the amazing plum of his tongue
sweetens my brain.
He is like nobody
since I love him.
His cock sinks deep
in my heart.

I have owed you a letter
for months.

I wanted to chide
the manner of your death
the way I might have once
revised your poem.

You are like nobody
since I love you,
& you are gone.

Can you believe
your death gave birth to me?
Live or die,
you said insistently.
You chose the second
& the first chose me.
I mourned you
& I found him
in one week.

Is love the sugar-coated poison
that gets us in the end?
We spoke of men
as often as of poems.
We tried to legislate away
the need for love —
that backseat fuck
& death caressing you.

Why did you do it
in your mother's coat?
(I know
but also know
I have to ask.)
Our mothers get us hooked,

then leave us cold,
all full-grown orphans
hungering after love.

You loved a man who spoke
'like greeting cards.'
'He fucks me well
but I can't talk to him.'
We shared that awful need
to talk in bed.
Love wasn't love
if we could only speak
in tongues.

& the intensity of unlove
increased
until the motor, the running motor
could no longer power
the driver,
& you, with miles to go,
would rather sleep.

Between the pills, the suicide pills
& our giggly vodkas in the Algonquin . . .
Between your round granny glasses
& your eyes blue as glaciers . . .
Between your stark mother-hunger
& your mother courage,

you knew there was only one poem
we all were writing.

No competition.
'The poem belongs to everyone
& God.'
I jumped out of your
suicide car
& into his arms.
Your death was mine.
I ate it
& returned.

Now I sit by a lake
writing to you.
I love a man
who makes my fingers ache.
I type to you
off somewhere in the clouds.
I tap the table
like a spiritualist.

Sex is a part of death;
that much I know.
Your voice was earth,
your eyes were glacier-blue.
Your slender torso
& long-stemmed American legs
drape across
this huge blue western sky.

I want to tell you 'Wait,
don't do it yet.'
Love is the poison, Anne,
but love eats death.

Acknowledgements

The following poems were first published in *Poetry*: 'Where It Begins', 'The Wives of Mafiosi'. Parts of 'Fruits & Vegetables' and 'The Objective Woman' first appeared in *Twen* (West Germany) in German translation; in *About Women: An Anthology of Contemporary Fiction Poetry and Essays*, edited by Stephen Berg and S. J. Marks Fawcett, 1973: 'Becoming a Nun'; in *American Poetry Review*: 'Gardener', 'Half-Life', 'For Claudia, Against Narrowness'; in *Aphra*: 'The Send Off'; in *Beloit Poetry Journal*: 'Tapestry, with Unicorn' (appeared in a somewhat different form under the name Erica Mann); in *Columbia Forum*: 'The Woman Who Loved To Cook'; in *Cosmopolitan*: 'Touch', 'Purification'; in *Encounter*: 'Colder'; in *Harper's*: 'Back To Africa'; in *Mountain Moving Day: Poems by Women,* edited by Elaine Gill, The Crossing Press, 1973: 'Colder', 'Sunjuice', 'In the Penile Colony', 'Becoming a Nun'; in *Ms*: 'Dear Marys, Dear Mother, Dear Daughter', 'Paper Cuts', 'Mother', 'Gardener'; in *The Nation*: 'Seventeen Warnings in Search of a Feminist Poem', 'Anniversary'; in *New York Quarterly*: 'Men'; in *Paris Review*: 'Becoming a Nun', 'From the Country of Regrets'; in *Ramparts*: 'How-to Books & Other Absurdities', 'Statue'; in *Redbook*: 'For My Husband', 'Penis Envy'. Other poems were previously published in the following periodicals: *Intro, # 3, Mademoiselle* and *The Southern Review*.

Two lines from 'Song' by Nicholas Moore, from *The Island and the Cattle*, © Nicholas Moore 1942, published by The Fortune Press. Six lines from 'Under the Maud Moon', from *The Book of Nightmares*, © Galway Kinnell 1971, published by Houghton Mifflin Company.

Bestselling Transatlantic Fiction in Panther Books

THE SOT-WEED FACTOR	John Barth	£1.50 ☐
BEAUTIFUL LOSERS	Leonard Cohen	60p ☐
THE FAVOURITE GAME	Leonard Cohen	40p ☐
TARANTULA	Bob Dylan	50p ☐
DESOLATION ANGELS	Jack Kerouac	50p ☐
THE DHARMA BUMS	Jack Kerouac	40p ☐
BARBARY SHORE	Norman Mailer	40p ☐
AN AMERICAN DREAM	Norman Mailer	40p ☐
THE NAKED AND THE DEAD	Norman Mailer	60p ☐
THE BRAMBLE BUSH	Charles Mergendahl	40p ☐
TEN NORTH FREDERICK	John O'Hara	50p ☐
FROM THE TERRACE	John O'Hara	75p ☐
OURSELVES TO KNOW	John O'Hara	60p ☐
THE DICE MAN	Luke Rhinehart	95p ☐
COCKSURE	Mordecai Richler	60p ☐
ST URBAIN'S HORSEMAN	Mordecai Richler	50p ☐
THE CITY AND THE PILLAR	Gore Vidal	40p ☐
BLUE MOVIE	Terry Southern	60p ☐
BREAKFAST OF CHAMPIONS	Kurt Vonnegut Jr	60p ☐
SLAUGHTERHOUSE 5	Kurt Vonnegut Jr	50p ☐
MOTHER NIGHT	Kurt Vonnegut Jr	40p ☐
PLAYER PIANO	Kurt Vonnegut Jr	50p ☐
GOD BLESS YOU, MR ROSEWATER	Kurt Vonnegut Jr	50p ☐
WELCOME TO THE MONKEY HOUSE	Kurt Vonnegut Jr	75p ☐

Bestselling British Fiction in Panther Books

Bestselling European Fiction in Panther Books

QUERELLE OF BREST	Jean Genet	60p	☐
OUR LADY OF THE FLOWERS	Jean Genet	50p	☐
FUNERAL RITES	Jean Genet	50p	☐
DEMIAN	Hermann Hesse	40p	☐
THE JOURNEY TO THE EAST	Hermann Hesse	40p	☐
LA BATARDE	Violette Leduc	60p	☐
THE TWO OF US	Alberto Moravia	50p	☐
THE LIE	Alberto Moravia	75p	☐
COMMAND AND I WILL OBEY YOU			
	Alberto Moravia	30p	☐
THE HOTEL ROOM	Agnar Mykle	40p	☐
THE DEFENCE	Vladimir Nabokov	40p	☐
THE GIFT	Vladimir Nabokov	50p	☐
THE EYE	Vladimir Nabokov	30p	☐
NABOKOV'S QUARTET	Vladimir Nabokov	30p	☐
INTIMACY	Jean-Paul Sartre	60p	☐
THE AIR CAGE	Per Wästberg	60p	☐

All these books are available at your local bookshop or newsagent, or can be ordered direct from the publisher. Just tick the titles you want and fill in the form below.

Name ....

Address ....

....

Write to Panther Cash Sales, PO Box 11, Falmouth, Cornwall TR10 9EN

Please enclose remittance to the value of the cover price plus:

UK: 18p for the first book plus 8p per copy for each additional book ordered to a maximum charge of 66p

BFPO and EIRE: 18p for the first book plus 8p per copy for the next 6 books, thereafter 3p per book

OVERSEAS: 20p for first book and 10p for each additional book

Granada Publishing reserve the right to show new retail prices on covers, which may differ from those previously advertised in the text or elsewhere.